SONNETS TO CRAIG

For Craig George.
from
Aug. 20th, 1911.

Sonnets
to
Craig

By
GEORGE STERLING
With Introduction by
UPTON SINCLAIR

AMS PRESS
NEW YORK

105383

Reprinted from the edition of 1928, Long Beach
First AMS EDITION published 1970
Manufactured in the United States of America

International Standard Book Number: 0-404-06259-8

Library of Congress Card Catalog Number: 78-119658

AMS PRESS, INC.
NEW YORK, N.Y. 10003

PREFACE

MANY strange experiences have been imagined by poets and woven into sonnet sequences; but few of them stranger than the story contained in the metal box which rests now upon the writer's desk. It holds letters and sonnets written many years ago to the woman who is now his wife, by the man who was then, and remained to the end, his dearest friend.

"Craig," as she is called in these poems, was born in the far South, the eldest child of an honored family. She was gifted with beauty of that rare kind which expresses the soul within. Beethoven is quoted as saying that he would like to break a certain woman's heart, in order that she might be able to sing; and the fates treated Craig according to this cruel formula, by a youthful love-affair and engagement which ended in tragedy. For five or six years thereafter she lived for her family, expecting no happiness of her own.

At the age of twenty-five she came to New York, with the manuscript of a partly completed biography of Winnie Davis, "the Daughter of the Confederacy." Soon after this she met George Sterling. The meeting took place in a drawing-room, and when George saw her, he stared, and then, without being introduced, or even knowing her name, went upon his knees before her, and caught her hand and kissed it. To quote his own words, written a few days later: "One glance, and the mischief was done. I was lost, and bound, and helpless as a babe. in the matter."

Craig had come North for the purpose of investigating the "literary world;" and here was a celebrated poet. What was a poet? And what was the meaning of his strange behavior? She had been trained in that art which in the South is called "coquetry," and to this new admirer

3

she said, at the outset, "Beware of me, I am a flirt; I pretend to be interested in men, but it's only to see what they are like, to make them pour out their hearts." George, reading in her shining eyes the truth, that she was the tenderest soul he had ever known, replied, "I am not afraid of you. I give you permission. Do what you will." Soon she said, "I cannot love you. There are many reasons, which I cannot even tell you." He answered, "It is enough to know that you exist. You have given me back my art." He went on to explain that strange thing, new to her, the soul of an artist. "I too have a game that I play. I put emotions into beautiful words. Let me pretend that you love me. You pretend it also, if you will. Do not be afraid of hurting me—the risk is mine."

Again and again he said this; and so the game was played, and every day there came letters, wild and tempestuous—"himmelhoch jauchzend, zum Tode betruebt"—amazing utterances to a daughter of the far South, who had never before in her life been anywhere without a chaperone. But she was determined to understand the modern world; being in rebellion against her old environment, the tragedy which had wrecked her girlhood, and the policy of shutting one's eyes to painful facts.

George went back to California, with the hope that Craig would come there, to visit her great-aunt. A few of the sonnets had been written in the East, but most of them came from California, where he waited and pleaded for months in vain. It happened that through a series of accidents Craig was witnessing from the inside a domestic tragedy which made what is called a "front page story." More aspects of the modern world, incredible to a daughter of the far South! She had met another writer, one who was at war with the "art for art's sake" formulas of George Sterling. The old duel between art

4

and propaganda, waged now in the soul of a woman. Which kind of work did she prefer? Which kind of life would she live?

George knew about this duel, and many times his letters voiced his fears. "I cannot foresee what illusive dreams may come to you. You may even conceive it your duty to marry Upton! I know now (at least I've a notion of) your capacity for idealistic self-sacrifice, and the thought of what your idealism and sympathy may lead you to is terrifying to me." And again: "I suppose that Upton is by now making frantic appeals to you to marry him. *Don't!* You two would never get along together; for though you are so willing to sacrifice yourself, he would be so willing to *let* you, that in the end your soul would revolt, and you would be most unhappy. *Both* should sacrifice, if such become necessary. But a man should be able to make sacrifice seem a joyous and irresistible thing—a completion and reward." Again he refers to Upton as "an ethical machine," who would turn Craig into the same evil thing.

The duel between art and propaganda was lost by art. Craig did not come to California to visit the great-aunt, but went to Europe—which is another story. George Sterling became an elder brother and devoted friend during the fifteen years of life that remained to him. He visited us for several weeks in Croton, and a number of times during our ten years in Pasadena. In all those years he never voiced a word of reproach, but watched, silently and despairingly, his "star in alabaster" functioning as "an ethical machine," and wrecking itself in the process. Now he is gone; and Craig looks back over the years, and it seems to her that the poet's life was one of the prices she paid for Socialist agitation. "No one who has not lived that life can imagine the stress and terror of it, perpetual and incessant"—so she exclaims. "It drains the blood and nerves, and leaves no time nor mind for personal relationships." And then, of course, come vain regrets. "A little more love and attention from me, and he might have been saved! One 'crusade' the less against social injustice, and the time given to a great poet!"

George is gone, and only the metal box full of letters and sonnets remains. So long as life and art both exist, life may claim precedence; but in the end there is only art, and it has its way. These poems might, of course, be issued anonymously: "Sonnets to a Lady," or something like that. But the name "Craig" is woven through them, an unusual name. To publish them without explanation would merely cause the reader to waste time in futile guessing, and it seems more sensible and straightforward to set forth these facts.

Only two persons know them, and one of the two is helpless. Craig cannot even read the sonnets for her tears. Left to herself she would keep the metal box in its concrete store-room. But among the letters is a statement from George: "They will be for you an enduring record of the fineness and worth of our love. And some day, when doing so can hurt neither yourself nor another, you may give them to the world." Also, she hears the argument of her husband, that great emotions, expressed in beautiful language, are more important than personal feelings. George Sterling's poetry is part of our literary heritage, and not the property of any individual.

George was a fastidious critic of all poetry, including his own; therefore his opinion of the sonnets is worth quoting. From Carmel he wrote: "I've a dozen poems for you, but all half-written. I will send you one each day, as I complete them. I feel like a singing god in robes of light and flame. The silence of six months is broken, and I am free, with swifter voice than ever, with wilder heart and stronger wings than I ever dared hope to possess. Wait, Craig! Wait! I'll sing such songs to you as never woman wrung in ecstasy from a man's heart in all the years of art. That is not a boast—not even an inducement: it is a prayer that you may save my soul alive and keep me from the ashes from which it sprang the instant I saw your face."

Again from Carmel, George comments: "I don't want you to think that because I can write so many sonnets they're not good ones. I hate to seem in the least boastful; and I do not think that I *am*. . . . For it is no credit to me to have set them down: something far greater than I is speaking through me, and at *your* direct inspiration. In giving, ultimately, this much beauty to the world, you and I are in the truest sense collaborators, each of no avail without the other. And I thank you."

How did it seem in the cold light of her marriage to another man? There is a fragment of a letter, undated, saying, "I spend most of the evening hours reading. Last night I reread my sonnets to you. But it was knives in the heart to see them again. I should never have gone back to them, feeling as I do! Nor should I write even this."

A few words as to the text of the letters and sonnets. They are written on many different kinds of paper, the envelopes bearing many postmarks—New York City, Sag Harbor, and then, en route to California; Carmel, where the poet had a cottage in the pines; San Francisco, where he stayed at the Bohemian Club; Oakland, where for a few weeks he was in his uncle's employ; and Glen Ellen, at the Jack London ranch. The period of the writing was less than one year. All the sonnets are in George's handwriting; none is typed. All but a few form part of the text of letters. None of these letters is dated, except with the day of the week; the places given here are derived from the postmark on the envelope, from the context, or from a comparison of the stationery. The sonnets have been placed in order of time, so far as this can be determined. In one letter George wrote that he had completed a "cycle"; we have found exactly one hundred, and two poems not sonnets. The letters mention by name two sonnets which have not been found. We have ventured to change the titles in several cases where two sonnets bore the same title.

The publication rights to this work have been purchased from the estate of George Sterling, his sisters.

CONTENTS

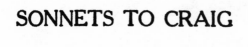

SONNETS TO CRAIG

I

REPENTANCE

How shall I face thy soul?—I, dumb and blind
  Before the holy beauty of thy face!
  Stand back from me! Have mercy for a space,
Lest madness break thine image in my mind!
For now I reach, who never dreamt to find,
  The ineffable, the utmost shrine of grace,
  Ere Time of all my worship leave no trace,
And this my heart be dust upon the wind.

Thy mercy for a while! This voice to thee
  Is out of darkness and unhallowed years.
    How shall my fire against thy snows be set?
I call as tho, to love that could not be,
  A fallen seraph wrote in his own tears
    His hopeless tale of heavenly regret.

Sag Harbor.

II

THY PICTURE

Withold, O God! the guerdon of my sight
  Or of Thy mercy grant me strength to bear
  This final dream of beauty unaware,
This star of stars in all the mortal night!
Alas! her utter loveliness! What might
  Shall draw me from the live and fragrant snare
  Of her effacing and elysian hair?
Nay! let me die there, lost within her light!

God, shall I not go mad, who know too well
That past these gates of fair and glorious dwell
  Divinities of soul surpassing all
    That sight shall ever fathom of her grace?
  Alas! what voices of enchantment call
    To Love grown sad with gazing on her face!

Sag Harbor.

III

TO CRAIG

I need not now a vision's light and pow'r
  To tell what loveliness was their's of old,
  When Egypt's siren with her lures untold
Or Helen leaning from her eastern tow'r
Or Rosamund within her hidden bow'r
  The lords and kingdoms of the world controlled.
  Those were but dross before thy magic gold,
Earth to thy pearl, and nettles to thy flow'r.

All gracious things and delicate and sweet
Within the spaces of thy beauty meet:
  God hath set mystic jewels in thine eyes,
    And in thy face the rose of all romance,
    And in thy lyric voice, beyond mischance,
  Such chords as wake for Love in Paradise.

Sag Harbor.

IV

THE UNALTERABLE

Sweetly within my heart, hushed otherwise,
  Thy voice in crystal echo ever rings,
  A music wherewith insubstantial things
To wordless pain and hidden rapture rise.
Never can I attain thee! Love denies
  His reddest rose to him who saddest sings:
  His joy is to the joyous, and his wings
Falter and fail when Hope forsakes the skies.

Yet loss no more can matter: I have seen!
  Tho love and life deny me, thou art thou—
    Now with thy light my lonely heavens fill.
Oh! from thy secret tower earthward lean,
  To bless me with the glory of thy brow—
    A star my soul shall worship, and be still.

Sag Harbor.

V

FOREBODING

Sweet, in this love are terrors that beguile
  And joys that make a hazard of my breath.
  I seem as one whose pathway wandereth
Where deadly blooms make fair a tropic isle,
And fatal fragrance lureth, many a mile,
  The stranger to some gorgeous glade of death.
  I dream not of thee save my spirit saith:
"Thy life or doom are hidden by her smile."

Art thou enchantress of the Not-to-be?
  A Lilith that can slay without a kiss?
    Art crueller because thou art so fair?
I crave thy secret, lest, (unhappy me!)
  Too eager for the nectar of thy bliss,
    Thy scorn become my poison. Love, beware!

Sag Harbor.

VI

QUESTION

For this love's gage, what flower may we choose?
  Sweet, shall it be a waif of Eden's bloom,
  Or some strange blossom ministrant to doom
And fragrant of disaster? Shall it lose
It's soul in evening raptures, or refuse
  The calice of its passion to the gloom?
  Be found the rose of amorous perfume,
Or jasmine with the morning on her dews?

Behold! thy brow is whiter! Shall I dare
  To touch thy marble with a mortal hand
    Or brave the storms of Heaven at thy kiss?
My spirit is imprisoned unaware.
  I live a shadow in a haunted land.
    I did not know that love could be like this!

Sag Harbor.

VII

FROM THE GLOOM

As one who, wandering in doubt and pain,
   Where waters dark and winds of midnight moan
   In some far wilderness as yet unknown,
Peers out upon a wide and trackless plain
Thro night no moon nor friendly stars attain,
   And seeks a refuge or a signal shown,
   Till, baffled, desperate, astray, alone,
He sees at last a light across the rain,—

So I, in darkness that thou canst not dream
   Of late a wanderer, uplift mine eyes
   And tremble, by thy distant radiance drawn.
Across life's plain I watch thy mystic beam,
   My goal beneath the re-enchanted skies:
     What is it thou shalt grant me—dusk or dawn?

Sag Harbor.

VIII

LOST MUSIC

Sweet, thou dost take this heart in tender hands
  And crush therefrom a music ceaselessly;
  For when 'tis night those chords acknowledge thee,
And in the day thy deathless memory stands
Like some strange flower found 'mid desert sands.
  O wild, wan blossom! let thy fragrance be
  A rapture and a mystery to me,
Who reach thee from insufferable lands.

O fragile music, lost like winds that die!
  O lone, last flower, mute and fountainless,
    What strains shall tell my sorrow and thy grace?
Thou passest as a moon adown the sky—
  Thou who hast drained the world of loveliness
    And set the blinding glory in thy face!

Sag Harbor.

IX

RESURRECTION

How hath my heart become a sweet amaze!
  A thousand thoughts, each sweeter than the last,
  Regrets a thousand for the barren Past,
And hopes ten thousand for the future days—
Such hath my life become. On thee I gaze
  As holds a worshipper his eyes upcast
  To some fair saint; but lovelier, thou hast
No need of Heaven to shrine thee with its rays.

There lies a radiance upon thy brow,
Purer than aught in Paradise. Aye! thou
  Dost bring God near to me, and stun my soul
    With visions of His farther love and place,—
  With tyrant dreams that startle and control
    In surmise of thy beatific grace.

Sag Harbor.

X

THE HEART OF MUSIC

I murmur: "Craig!" At once in every vein
  There stirs a subtle and unresting fire
  Too wild to tame, too sorrowful to tire,—
So might God's saddest star cry out amain;
Such chords the flashing hands of Love attain,
  Bright at his breast the supplicating lyre,
  When Music, calling in supreme desire,
Tells to the night her glory and her pain.

Deep in my heart its echo sobs and dies,
And dying, leaves a darkness that mine eyes
  Search for a sign of thee, however vague.
    O sweet, lost strains! O voice of vanished wings!
    Again I turn me to immortal things:
    Again in ecstasy I murmur: "Craig!"

Sag Harbor.

XI

VERSES TO CRAIG

Oh! in the past, when I heard music call,
  Thy voice was in its crying!
Thy beauty, as I watched the sunsets fall,
  Was portion of their dying!

Yet could I know that all things led to thee?
That thou of all wast flower?
That thou wast lily of the days to be,—
  Rose of their hidden bower?

And art thou mortal, of a mortal born?
  For in thy face's lurings
Is loveliness more dear than that of morn
  Or twilights unenduring.

Thou seem'st to draw thy substance from the moon,
  Thy glance from starlight's gleaming,
And this thy breath seems jasmine warm with June,
  In glades where gods lie dreaming.

And in thee meet all ends of strange and fair,
  All grace and life and wonder—
A goddess-girl from lonely islands where
  Unresting billows thunder.

So, tell me thou art Circe come again,
  To grant, on some to-morrow,
All mirth and magic, loneliness and pain,
  All rapture and all sorrow.

Sag Harbor.

XII

PARTING

Darling, the wild, inexorable hour
  Came suddenly to birth, a bitter tear
  Upon the face of that enchanted Year
That made but now thy heart my holy dower
And mine thy fane forever. By its power
  The face that God hath made so very dear
  Is now a star on heavens remote and clear
And in my soul the one and perfect flower.

The thought of thee is silence to my pain;
  The thought of thee is pain and fiery wings
    That lift me to the skies of Love my lord.
What purity upon thy brow hath lain,
  And on thy lips what hint of wordless things!
    How beautiful! thou dearest! thou adored!

Chicago.

XIII

A PRAYER

God, Thou who bringest morning out of night,
    Bring her to me, so more to me than morn!
    Fair as those roses of Thine east reborn
From pure abysses of celestial light,
So let her steal on my adoring sight,
    So let her greet me, I who go forlorn,
    By wildest hope and fears unceasing torn,
Who, finding Love, have found him in his might.

But bring her not as morning comes, to *go,*
    Nor mock me with a fleeting Paradise,
    Tho in her face its holiest flowers live!
Yea! knowing her, what more remains to know?
    For I have gazed within her tender eyes,
    And found Thee there, and all thou hast to give!

En route to California.

XIV

LONELY

I saw but now a wild-dove and his mate
  Pass down the river on the morning blue;
  Above the willows' emerald they flew,
Bondless and swift, untroubled and elate.
Happy, I thought, happy their feathered fate,
  For they had sipped the dawn's elysian dew
  And found them autumn's tawny seeds a few,
While as for me, I starve, I grieve, I wait!

And thou, O Far One, in thy stony nest,
Thou too art lonely, gazing to the West.
  O thou mine exquisite and tender dove,
    Follow me, follow, for my hunger grows,
    And I would gaze again upon thy snows,
  Lost heavenward in a semi-swoon of love.

En route.

XV

AT THE GRAND CANYON

Thou settest splendors in my sight, O Lord!
  It seems as tho' a deep-hued sunset falls
  Forever on these Cyclopean walls,
These battlements where Titan hosts have warred,
And hewn the world with devastating sword,
  And shook with trumpets the eternal halls
  Where Seraphim lay hid by bloody palls
And only Hell and Silence were adored.

Lo! the abyss wherein the wings of Death
Might beat unchallenged, and his fatal breath
  Fume up in pestilence. Beneath the sky
    Is no such testimony unto grief.
    Here Terror walks with Beauty ere she die.
      Oh! hasten to me, Love, for life is brief!

XVI

AUTUMN

Ah! well I know that I shall never find
  Thy like this side of Heaven! Well I know
  That whether on the ways of dream I go,
Or seek thy semblance with awaken'd mind,
Naught can avail, and I as well were blind.
  About .thee lies the summer's afterglow,
  Where Autumn, lonely in her golden woe,
Hints of its secret with the homeless wind.

Tho' Heaven and hope forsake me, still thou art,
  And all my memory is made thy throne.
    O lonely in thy loveliness, be true!
O rose without a sister! close thy heart
  To all but me! Thy memory in mine own
    Hides like a tear of everlasting dew.

San Francisco.

XVII

ABSENCE

Thy beauty is an altar where I kneel,
  Thy soul the Heaven of my constant pray'r.
  Darling, I find thine image everywhere,
Thy lure in sunset and the moons that wheel
O'er evening valleys where their beams reveal
  Too much of loveliness for day to share.
  My soul is lost in thine. I wait aware
Of hopes too dear for Sorrow to conceal.

Alas the gulfs that hold thy breast from mine!
  Alas my heart, too high for lesser pain!
  I love thee, as they love who loving die!
I crave from Passion her ecstatic wine,
  From Love, the gardens that the gods attain,
  From Rapture, all her kisses ere she sigh.

San Francisco.

XVIII

WORSHIP

Deny me not forever, for in thee
  All beauty seems regathered and reborn
  Thou art that rose whose garden is the morn,
The pearl whose beauty haunts the dreamland sea,
And that romance whose immortality
  Endures our dreary planet but in scorn;
  For thee the lyres of Eden wait forlorn
Ere yet thy coming set their music free.

In what sincerity can I defend
  Mine art's insistence of thy loveliness,
    Tho' such be but the mortal shadow thrown
By soul on flesh! Before its light I bend
  As one who holds his kindred none the less,
    Yet who has worship for one face alone.

San Francisco.

XIX

HOMEWARD

O paths of stone, whereon the weary stray
  From toil to toil, from sin to tawdry sin,
  Farewell awhile! The silences begin
To call me to my kingdom far away.
There sings the lark to welcome back the day,
  And there the poppies in the moonlight thin
  Invite to dream, and there the pine-boughs win
A fitful music from the wind's delay.

Farewell! I hasten to the sapphire South,
  There to be lonely till my goddess come
To blind me with the kisses of her mouth;
    And I shall wander where the cypress broods,
  And listen as the bees of Carmel hum—
    A faun again in sacred solitudes.

Pajaro.

XX

THE KISS

Adored! adored! thy lips were on mine own
   Like fragrance tangible, or like a rose
   Nurtured by Love in Circe's garden-close,
Or blossom by his hands immortal sown;
And silence now to melody has grown,
   And music to enchanted silence flows;
   The winds are choral with unuttered woes;
The sea has hidden meanings in its moan.

So Artemis such joy in guerdon keeps,
   Husht, and descendant on celestial wings
   That mix their pearl with evening, as she brings,
     Where deep of Slumber's cup Endymion sips,
Her silver to the face of him who sleeps,
   Her passion to the unrealizing lips.

Carmel.

XXI

BY LONELY WATERS

Hope said: "These are the sands that she shall tread
   And this the sea whereon her gaze shall rest,
   For she shall seek thee in the lordly West.
In yonder woodlands shall her feet be led,
And as a lily shall she lay her head
   On thine impassioned and enchanted breast.
   She shall know all, and know that love is best,
Beside the ocean when the West is red."

Aye! so her music trembled at my heart
   And built in flame the Garden of my Dream,
    And died, and was a portion of the Past;
But ere those wings were lifted to depart,
   Her music blossomed to a note supreme—
    The cry of famished lips that meet at last.

Carmel.

XXII

PASSION'S HOUR

To-day the flesh contemns the craven mind
　And revels like a tiger in the sun;
　I drink the noon's elixir, and am one
With fauns that seek the Oreads, as I find
A passionate compulsion in the wind,
　Upon whose path the cloudland chariots run
　To some remote and airy Avalon,
Where Joy is crowned, nor any nymph unkind.

To-day the tender mystery of thy soul
Seems half-forgot, nor utterly my goal:
　I crave thy lips, I crave the flame thereof—
　　Mad for that hour of ecstasy and fire
　　In which the deathless pinions of Desire
　Are shadows on the semi-swoon of love.

Carmel.

XXIII

INTIMATION

O shall it be, O shall it be at last
   That thou wilt come with morning in thine eyes
   And lead me into utmost Paradise,
And with twain kisses seal forever fast
The portals to the miserable Past?
   Darling! thy holy face upon my skies
   Is evening star, and where the dawning lies
Thou art the star above its rose upcast!

Sweet, I have sought all visions fair and good,
   And seeking thro' the world have come to thee
   And known thee for my Eden evermore.
I seemed, when first before thy grace I stood,
   Like one who hears in dream beside the sea
   A surf of rapture on a spirit shore.

Carmel.

XXIV

SHADOWS OF THEE

How picture what thy beauty is to me?
  'Tis like a wine that laughing gods have crushed;
  A dream by some forgotten sunset flushed;
A fane of silver on a moonlit sea;
A morning ocean where the winds are free.
  'Tis like a garden by the twilight hushed;
  A bower where a perfect rose has blushed;
A sense of music from eternity.

Oh! all of loveliness by Nature blent
With lure and vision to the spirit lent
  Are but the symbols of thy goddesshood!
    Thou comest on the silence of my sleep
  As once at dawn the Cytherean stood
    A flame of splendor on the adoring deep!

Carmel.

XXV

THE UNATTAINABLE

In love's wild desperation of desire
  I seek thee, I adore thee! Sweet, my hands
  Would fain despoil high Paradise, or lands
Of rapture unattainable. I tire—
I and my dreams—before the vision dire
  Of thine infinitude. The mournful strands
  Of life's dim ocean reach their foam-set sands
For one white chord of Love's angelic lyre.

I cannot name thee. Lo! the hands of God,
  Moulding thy marvel, wrought my worshipping.
    Ah! what am I without thee, thou mine own?
The far, forgotten ways my feet have trod
  Had naught of worth nor honor save to bring
    This heart of adoration to thy throne.

Carmel.

XXVI

THE FONT OF BEAUTY

Because of thee the star-crost dome of night
  Adds love and rapture to infinity;
  Wherefore should sunsets burn, except that we
Drain to our souls the splendors of their flight?
With thee shall I tread Andes of delight
  Beneath my feet as mole-hills, till I see
  That God Himself is sure because of thee,
And thou and I dear children in His sight.

Thy hands have strewn the roses of the dawn;
  Thy face repays for every flower that dies;
  Thy whisper is the song Astarte sings!
Thy grace hath caught its silence from the faun;
  Thy heart hath stolen starlight from the skies;
  Thy spirit is the wind of Beauty's wings!

Carmel.

XXVII

HOPE'S PARADISE

How exquisitely, darling, art thou made
  For love! Thy body, all of pearl and rose,
  Hath passion's keenest rapture to disclose,
Tho' like a pure and perfect lily, laid
On Aphrodite's altar, ne'er to fade
  If Dian comes full-envious, and shows
  Her wannest lilies in the moonlight's snows.
Thou art Love's sun, as other loves his shade!

Ah! would that in a secret dusk we lay,
  On gathered hearts of Eden's whitest flow'rs,
    With ghosts of Eden's fragrance on the air,
Breast unto breast in swoon too sweet to say
  What ecstasy was blossom of the hours,
    What mystery was Love's supremest care!

Carmel.

XXVIII

THE SOUL-GIVER

O thou whose snows of body and of soul
   Compel I hold immaculate mine own,
   And live unsatisfied, and mourn alone
Where sea-winds grieve and sombre waters roll!
O thou my beacon-light and single goal,
   Whose breast has been, whose breast shall be, my
      throne!
   O star upon the Future's night unknown!
O dawn that comest, tho' the dark control!

Thine are the quiet sessions of my heart,
   And thine the peaceless surgings of its fire.
Nor may the solemn seraphim of Art
    Deny this love: thou too hast Heaven's youth—
   One thought of thee can make my soul aspire
    To all they serve of Beauty and of Truth!

Carmel.

XXIX

THE INEXORABLE HOUR

Methought the Spirit of the Night took form
　And stood before me with despotic brow,
　Crying: "Thy love's embrace allures thee now,
And now the haven of her breast is warm,
And still her star is empress of the swarm
　My wings o'ershadow.　Make her then thy vow.
　Still to the heavens of her beauty bow
And orbs the angels of my House shall storm!

Yea! list awhile the love-linkt words she saith,
　Which bar my dreadful music from thine ears;
But I am sister of unsparing Death,
　　And soon my hands shall hold her dust and thine—
　The harvest of annihilating years
　　When seas are stilled and suns no longer shine!"

Carmel.

XXX

AT THE LILY'S HEART

Within me (roguish brother!) lives a faun
  Demure as any whom Arcadian bees
  Made drowsy with their murmur, or the sea's
Far thunder woke on some Illyrian dawn;
And he the blue-eyed dryad on the lawn
  Would fain allure with woodland sorceries,
  But *thou* shalt see him on his bended knees,
O goddess by the bitter years withdrawn!

Lo! Passion here puts by her scarlet wreath,
  And yet abideth Passion. In thy kiss
  Nobility and rapture blend their hues
As stars might fashion in the flowers beneath
  A symbol of my worship and its bliss,
  Enmirrored for a night in earthly dews.

Carmel.

XXXI

THE JOYS UNCHANGING

The stars' communion, and the Night's pure pow'rs,
  The cry of Music and her mystery,
  The sweep and domination of the sea,
The ever-blessèd faces of the flow'rs
Lifted to Spring's reanimating show'rs,
  And Slumber's consolation, and the free
  Elysian winds—they mock satiety,
Nor loose their magic with the cloying hours.

From these Time steals no glory. As of old
Their bliss and charm depart not, but enfold,
  As vaster things, the spirit. Years efface
    Our pomps, but here no disenchantment mars.
  Remains one other thing that shares their grace:
    The words, "I love thee!" Such are as the stars.

Carmel.

46

XXXII

LOVE THE TRANSMUTER

I, who was lonely Beauty's loner priest.
  (If solitude of heart so testify),
  Stand loneliest now, with all that heart a sigh.
The music of the world has never ceast;
Still bloom the dawn's wide lilies on the east,
  And still the faces of the gods go by,
  But down at evening from the quiet sky,
When spirits muse, dream-held and dream-releast.

What sun has made Time's mystery a light,
  Simple and splendid as the litten Dew
By day-warm grasses gathered from the night?
    What golden spell is on familiar things,
  That all seem marvellously strange and new,—
    That sunset now seems thronged with heavenly wings?

Carmel.

XXXIII

SEARCH REWARDED

I waited thee thro sacrificial years,
  And till thou camest all my soul was blind.
  'Tis written, "He that seeketh, he shall find,"
And I have sought thy face in all the spheres,
Still haunted by the voice that no man hears
  Save from the Love unknown but well divined.
  O Rose beyond the questings of the wind!
O Star mine eyes must see thro many tears!

Thou art the silence in my soul, and thou
The kiss of things unseen upon my brow.
  O loveliness the sorrowed night hath dreamed
    And dawn found perfect! Harp of mystery
  Upon whose chords forgotten moons have gleamed,
    Within whose voice are voices of the sea!

Carmel.

XXXIV

BLISS DECREED

In all our love I find no touch of guilt:
  A sense of mornings delicate and pure
  Lingers therein, and mornings that endure,
Yet have their tears, like dew some rose hath spilt.
But night hath lesser mystery, nor wilt
  Thou find, O Music, evermore its lure,
  Altho' thou roam the palace insecure
By sunset on the western ocean built!

Not of ourselves is love so made supreme,
  And fostered with extremities of bliss,
    For suns and seas upon its service wait;
The gods ordain the enchantment of its dream,
  And past the blinding rapture of thy kiss
    Abides the hunger of the lips of Fate.

Carmel.

XXXV

THE BURDEN OF THE PAST

Fool that I was to dream I loved before!
  But now a sweeter worship lets me know
  What ghosts I followed in the long ago,
What weeds my heart's neglected garden bore,
Where now one rose is splendid evermore,
  And where I wander ministrant and slow,
  As those incomparable petals glow,
And give my soul their beauty o'er and o'er.

Craig, ever thus I wander and repent,
  Slave of a thousand ecstasies and fears,
    Too humble to be sure, too glad to flee,
And all too glad in love's one punishment—
  The heart's slow scorn, augmenting with the years,
    For all that had not birth and life in thee.

Carmel.

XXXVI

PAST FLESH AND SOUL

Darling, if ne'er again, yet listen now,
  Since now, forsaken of it all, I find
  'Tis not thy loveliness that holds me blind
To other beauty, as afar I bow
In faith and worship of a lover's vow,—
  Nay, nor the lure and riches of thy mind,
  The marvel of the spirit well-divined
That hath her throne of light within thy brow.

Ah! not for each perfection do I call
  Thy love my kingdom and thyself my queen,
    But for a deeper goddess still more dear,
The mystery and essence of them all,
  The inner Thou, untouched, unheard, unseen—
    A subtle flame, a music, yea—a tear!

Carmel.

XXXVII

SUNSET

Save of the heart there is no loneliness,
   And thou hast made mine own one ache for thee—
   A subtle pain, a bliss exalting me
Till memory is made thy wild caress.
Heaven is no more, and earth can be no less,
   Nor any dream of either cease to be
   Thy lure, thy meaning and thy mystery,
With joys that rack, and agonies that bless.

Ere twilight strike the golden fields to grey,
I murmur "Craig! Beloved!" to the day,
   Till all the world is music to my heart.
      Yea! till from soundless peaks of western flame
   I seem to hear, O goddess that thou art!
      The dying lips of Sunset breathe thy name.

Carmel.

XXXVIII

LOVE'S COMPANION

Thy memories are seraphs that abide:
  This has thy smile to welcome me, and this
  The immeasurable rapture of thy kiss;
For all the radiant band seems but allied
To hold my heart in Paradise and guide
  My feet on all its ways of final bliss;
  And well I know at last I shall not miss
The throning path that leads me to thy side.

And then—and then! Oh! pure, impassioned lips!
  O blossoms that my very heart hath kist!
    How shall I touch, nor crush, your tenderness,
From which all fragrance into music slips,
  Till earth and sky seem only to exist
    To shrine you, making Heaven itself the less?

Carmel.

XXXIX

LOVE'S SHADOW

Great love is ever sorrow. In some way
  I cannot picture but must always feel,
  Grief to great love is sacrament and seal—
On love's blue dome a distant cloud of grey;
A hush beyond the music of the day;
  A tabernacle pure where mourners kneel;
  A sunset fair on which the night shall steal;
Belovèd starlight that the dawn shall slay.

Ah! we who love, think not that we shall miss
  That sense of things too lovely to endure!
  For souls that know, as thine, his gracious lure,
  The seraph Sorrow hath his hidden skies,
And when I gain thy lips I somehow kiss
  That lonely angel of the solemn eyes.

Carmel.

XL

AT DUSK

Eve, and the stainèd pinions of the day,
  Far-sinking as an eagle to her nest
  On some encrimsoned isle beyond the West.
But o'er thy distant and imagined way
I know the stars inexorable lay
  Their spell upon the night, the night unblest
  That bars me from the haven of thy breast,
And all the joy my soul would swoon to say.

Oh! sad as morning fled or twilight come
  The weeks and days that part my lips from thine,
Whose murmurs hold the chords of Eden dumb,
  As now in memory's regretful night
  I build and enter an enchanted shrine—
  Thy voice its music and thy face its light!

Carmel.

XLI

THE SPIRIT OF DUSK

Now the wide splendors of the lapsing sun
  Enfold me and my sunset dream of thee.
  Before my gaze the troubling of the sea
Abideth not, passing like sunset done.
Me the grey wings of fleeting Twilight shun,
  Where lost I roam in golden dreams of thee,
  Taking no part in night. I wander free,
Not in despair, yet with Love's sorrow one.

Unseen of dusk, Love walketh at my side,
  With eyes that close in mercy of my pain—
    Dear eyes mine own no longer may endure.
The night hath claspt the ocean in its tide
  And showered the shaken stars upon the main—
    White as our love, and as thy spirit pure.

Carmel.

XLII

THE COMING SINGER

The Veil before the mystery of things
  Shall stir for him with iris and with light;
  Chaos shall have no terror in his sight
Nor earth a bond to chafe his urgent wings;
With sandals beaten from the crown of kings
  He shall tread down the altars of their night,
  And stand with Silence on her breathless height,
To hear what song the star of morning sings.

With perished beauty in his hands as clay,
  Shall he restore futurity its dream.
Behold! his feet shall take a heavenly way
    Of choric silver and of chanting fire,
  Till in his hands unshapen planets gleam,
    'Mid murmurs from the Lion and the Lyre.

Carmel.

XLIII

EROS IN HEAVEN

Our love is all of crystal and of fire:
  The body's scarlet and the spirit's white
  Take as a star their splendor from the night,
Which is Love's day. So ere his day expire,
Ah! lead me to that Heaven of high desire
  Where soul and body gain the final height—
  Welded in dumb convulsions of delight—
To which unmingled they in vain aspire.

Oh! harken, on the silences of Fate,
The god within me calling to his mate,
  And with thy madnesses accord to me,
    Whom visions cheat and fantasies enmesh,
  The fierce, inseparable ecstasy,—
    The fury of the joy-tormented flesh!

Carmel.

XLIV

THE STAR OF SEPARATION

Darling, my heart seems now an empty sky,
  And thou the lonely star for which it waits,
  Ere Twilight loose the dim, celestial gates
And, purely shed, thy rays of beauty fly
To one whose very life endures thereby—
  Who finds therein the challenge of the Fates,
  Pain that exalts, and love that consecrates
The body's hunger and the spirit's sigh.

Not to *thine* evening shall the moon lend lure,
  Who art diviner magic, as the looms
    Of darkness weave their splendors in thy zone!
Here where the voices of the deep endure
  I watch thy glory on the pathless glooms,
    Adoring thee, adoring thee alone.

Carmel.

XLV

A MIDNIGHT

The silent and insufferable night
  Lies round me like the sea about its dead.
  My hopes are fostered and my heart is fed
By gleam and glamour of thy face's light,
My final star of Fate and meed of sight.
  Thy love is like a glory round my head—
  A moon undarkened and a splendor shed
From life's last pinnacle and breathless height.

Ah! dearest! that my passion and its fire
  Might wrap thy bosom in ecstatic flame,
And crush thee to the breast of my desire,
  In rapture all too vast for song to name!
    Yea! till we cried with compensated breath:
    "God! I have *lived!* release me now to death!"

Carmel.

XLVI

TRANSMUTATION

Thine alchemy hath touched familiar things
　And made of each a fairer than I know;
　For now when music wakens, 'tis as tho'
Thy soul had spoken.　Never linnet sings
But what my heart flies forth on wilder wings
　Than his; and when the winds in whispers go,
　From gardens where thou art they seem to blow,
And weave thy voice amid their murmurings.

And in each other sense my heart hath found
All that thy subtle magic gives to sound;
　For sight hath memories exquisite with thee,
　　And past all bliss of Heaven mad with bliss—
Ah! past its deepest dream of ecstasy!—
　　Sink on my lips the roses of thy kiss.

Carmel.

XLVII

GOD'S LILY

A dream within a dream: it seemed I slept
  Beneath the shadows of a moon-washed glade,
  With lilies in my arms benignly laid—
Found in a valley where the dusk had wept;
Star-pale was each, from out whose calice crept
  A fragrance that was soul of slumber's shade
  And spirit of its silence, as it made
My breast a harp that dreamland fingers swept.

And then I dreamt I woke, but mine embrace
  No longer knew the holy lilies' gleam,
For whiter, purer, thou hadst found their place,
  And sweeter on my lips thy loving breath!
  O crowning, O unutterable dream!
    Return it, Heaven! altho' the cost be death!

Carmel.

XLVIII

FROM DAWN TO DREAM

Soul of the world! my Paradise and dream!
  Now dawn makes all my heart one purest fane
  Wherein the marvel of thy face again
Hath glory past the sun's rerisen beam.
Devout and bowed, to thee, adored, supreme,
  I make the orison of Love's sweet pain—
  A low and incommunicable strain,
Sung by the soul where Love's white altars gleam.

Till evening clasp the world, and shadows dumb
  Rebuild the palace of the night, and thou
    Turn softly as the twilight to thy rest;
Till on the verge of dream my soul shall come
  And lay with sleep my kiss upon thy brow,
    As dew that sinks upon a lily's breast.

Carmel.

XLIX

FIRE OF DREAMS

Dearest, didst thou in spirit all the night
  Lie in mine arms? For ceaselessly I burned,
  A famished star made desperate, and yearned
To thee below the constellations' flight.
O mocking Vision, marvellous and white!
  Caught in thy toils intangible I turned,
  Still by the flawless feet of Rapture spurned
From pinnacles in Edens of delight!

I would that morning might awhile efface
The pain of that immaculate embrace!
  Alas! thy lips were bitter on mine own!
    Thy limbs denied me and thy fragrant breast!
  Thou spakest to me, in a tongue unknown,
    Impassioned incantations of unrest!

Carmel.

L

THY CHILD-PICTURE

O gentlest beauty! pure, untroubled face!
  O breaking bud, unmarred by grief and fear!
  What dews were thine from Heaven? what waters clear
From earth? what zephyrs in thy sheltered place
Nurtured thy delicate and girlish grace?
  What smile of innocence, what firstling tear,
  Told that a joy or sorrow waited near
Whose hands as yet could leave so secret trace?

Across what years that pensive gaze hath come,
  To find at last its haven in my breast!
  O dear child-face! O vision tenderest
Of all the dreams of Time! thou holdest dumb
  My lips a little—how could I divine
  That I should tremble nearest Heaven at thine?

Carmel.

LI

EVANESCENCE

I muse upon the passing of the days:
   Sunset has fled, and all the gracious land
   Lies in a trance of twilight, as I stand
Before the evening stars uplifted rays.
It floats above the purple ocean-ways
   As pure, as lone as thou. But here the strand
   Bears not thy footprints on its glimmering sand—
The very star is drifting from my gaze.

Love, all things pass—tell me thou wilt not go!
   For what is life without thee? what am I?
     Ah! Sweet! within the lost Hesperides
To walk with thee where winds of sorrow blow,
   When harps to unreturning sunsets cry
     The loneliness of stars, the grief of seas!

Carmel.

LII

SORROW AND JOY

Sweet, as above thy written words I bend
  Thou gleamest in a victory of tears.
  I gaze, I doubt, nor dare to doubt; the years
Have blossomed all too swiftly to this end
I meet so ill prepared: bright blisses rend
  My soul that burned alone; too soon it hears
  The music born of love's transcendent fears,—
Too soon it finds the heart's Eternal Friend!

Abide thou peacefully upon the throne
My hopes upbuild thee in the white Unknown!
  Gaze heavenward—there are no skies like these!
    Thy passion bears me to a mystic land
    Wherein is naught of life except I stand
  Lord of thy sorrows and thine ecstasies.

Carmel.

LIII

BEAUTY AFAR

Love, it is moonlight in thy heavens now,
But here the sunset lingers in the west
Like scarlet domes of Avalon the Blest.
I stand beside the sea and dream that thou
Upholdest to the moon thy whiter brow,
And all my soul upflames in holy quest
Of words to tell thy beauty, till my breast
Is like a shrine where choral angels bow.

Her scattered pearls seem centered in thy face;
She robes thee in a pure and lustrous rain.
Love! I beseech thee from as far a place
And ask thy mercy for a day unknown,
Abiding at the gates of Heaven in vain,
For oh! I enter by thy kiss alone!

Carmel.

LIV

FROM ARCADY

Goddess and holder of my heart in pawn!
  Hasten to me, for deep in Carmel pines
  Are dryad quietudes and shadowy shrines
Secluded for the worship of the faun.
O come! and we adown some moonlit lawn
  Will dance, and grace our brows with tawny vines,
  Where Autumn pours a witchery of wines
And ferny hollows wait the feet of Dawn.

And deeper yet amid the ancient trees
  There lies a bower that no foot has trod
    These many years—a couch whereon to dare
The stress and marvel of such ecstasies
  As never yet love's goddess and a god
    Woke on a bed of asphodel to share.

Carmel.

LV

LONELIEST

Thou biddest that my tears withhold their rain
  And askest Hope to be mine hourly guest,
  Undoubted, merciful: as well request
That I be glad yet know this love in vain!
Ah God! to find at last their blissful pain—
  The lips, the arms, the white angelic breast!
  Ah God! in that pure Paradise to rest
Nor dream of doubt and loneliness again!

Yet sings not Hope most like that timid thrush
  Whose voice is sweetest in a wilderness?
    In subtler things what rapture still can be!
The delicate, unfathomable flush
  That haloes perfect sunsets—thy caress—
    Thy smile—thy voice—thine eyes' divinity!

Carmel.

LVI

BELOVÈD

As music out of silence, Craig, so came
  Thy love from mystery; so, darling, now
  The lilies are less radiant than thy brow,
On which my heart beholds celestial flame.
Thou art all white, my queen; there is no name
  In all the lore of love for such as thou;
  The moon's wan breast, the foam beneath the prow,
The cherry bloom—thou bringest them to shame!

Thou art *too* fair! How shall I worship thee,
  Thou sister of the dawn? How cry thy praise?
  Nay! tho' I sing thro' many dusks and days
I cannot tell with words thy gift to me,
  Who, ere Heaven's crystal gleamed beneath my feet,
  Hast made the tale of all its bliss complete.

Carmel.

LVII

HESPERIA

What spoils of perfectness from far and wide
  Were gathered for thy full perfectitude!
  What blossoms delicate and subtly-hued,
And nacre from the moon's unsullied side,
Upon thy maiden countenance abide!
  And on thy mouth lost roses are renewed
  And in thine eyes celestial light is dewed.
Ah! that thy voice might live what music died!

Thou art the sum of all, and final sweet
Of all fair things made hopelessly complete.
  Thy feet on deathless asphodels are led;
    Thou waitest where the gates of vision are,
  With Heaven a golden mist beyond thy head,
    As lies the sunset round the evening star.

Carmel.

LVIII

THE ETERNAL VISITANT

Love, of whose bliss I dreamt, at last is mine,
  Mine evermore in fealty to guard,
  Mine evermore to contemplate unmarred,
Knowing its domination is divine.
O gracious sanctuary! lonely shrine
  Whose roof with orbs of amethyst is starred,
  Whose gate with gold and crysophrase is barred,
Before whose blaze the swords angelic shine!

These many years I sought thee, holy flame—
  Thou star of evening o'er the purple walls
    Of dreamland cities girdled by the deep!
Thou comest now as lucently as came
  Endymion's moon, and tenderly as falls
    The kiss of Silence on the brows of Sleep.

Carmel.

LIX

KINDRED

Musing, between the sunset and the dark,
  As Twilight in unhesitating hands
  Bore from the faint horizon's underlands,
Silvern and chill, the moon's phantasmal ark,
I heard the sea, and far away could mark
  Where that unalterable waste expands
  In sevenfold sapphire from the mournful sands,
And saw beyond the deep a vibrant spark.

There sank the sun Arcturus, and I thought:
  Star, by an ocean on a world of thine,
    May not a being, born, like me, to die,
Confront a little the eternal Naught
  And watch our isolated sun decline—
    Sad for his evanescence, even as I?

San Francisco.

LX

EVENING MUSIC

The myriad voicèd twilight clasps me round,
  As day in its encompassing decline
  For flowers that shone repays with stars that shine.
The splendid afternoon renounced all sound
That now in woodland maze or meadow's bound
  Rings from the grass or murmurs in the pine.
  O gracious hour! O gloaming half-divine!
O hush of noon by evening music crowned!

Better this peace than all the pulsing day,
  But best a voice that day nor twilight brings—
    Softer than noons made mournful by the dove,
Sweeter than harps when maiden hands delay,
  High as the song that Sappho's spirit sings—
    The Heaven and music of thy whisper, Love!

Carmel.

LXI

LOVE AND JOY

Oh! doubt not Love can live on dreams alone,
  If so they be forevermore of thee!
  From frailest hope he draws sweet certainty,
Seizing the wingèd bliss before 'tis flown,
Plucking the blossom ere the seed be sown,
  And crushing wine from clusters yet to be.
  Despair itself becomes an ecstasy,
And tears diviner things than Peace hath known.

Ever upon the gloom he sees the star,
  And steals To-day's uncompensated flow'rs
    To cast before To-morrow's glimmering feet.
His bride is Joy, altho she roam afar,
  Whose laughter on the inestimable hours
    Falls from the heavens wherein her wings are fleet.

San Francisco.

LXII

DOUBT AND WORSHIP

To search thy heart! to know thine every thought!
  Craig, art thou yearning for me, that I find
  Thy voice alone upon the unresting wind,
And, subtly in departing beauty caught,
Hints of thy purer loveliness untaught
  In Love's high lore, to Love's betrayal blind,
  Yet dare I serve him, he who holds enshrined
All tears and raptures that my heart hath sought.

O Sweet! thou rose whose thorn is ecstasy!
The garden of the world is fair with thee,
  Of countless worlds who wast the rose supreme
    Ere yet the fleeting bubble of our own
    With breath of dark Infinity was blown—
Who shalt be flower of Eden and its dream!

San Francisco.

LXIII

LOVE'S SACRAMENT

How high the Dreams that in thy spirit wake!
  I cannot deem thee made alone for bliss,
  Tho' better instant death than that I miss
The raptures in thy keeping, and forsake
  Such joys immeasurable as could break
A god's deep heart with ecstasy like this.
Thy maiden arms, thy ravishing, slow kiss—
  Ah! dearest! dearest! proffer that I take!

Yet must I take upon my bended knee,
  Lest the twain seraphs in our bosoms weep
    And human touch not lips with the divine.
How shall I know of Heaven apart from thee?—
  Thou for whom nights are wide and oceans deep!
    Thou for whose soul Infinity is shrine!

Carmel.

LXIV

DIVINITY

Sweet is this hunger of my flesh for thine,
  Which, if it feed, must feed on dreams alone;
  Yet tho thy lips shut flame upon mine own,
Still were the dreadful ecstasy divine.
Yea! tho thy lilied breast were set to mine
  And all thy beauty given me for throne,
  Yet were the sacrament till then unknown—
The body's bread, the soul's immortal wine.

Abides no other like thee, Craig! Till now
  To gods of clay and shrines unlit I knelt,
    Nor knew the Love whose feet in Heaven have trod.
Surely his kiss was holy on thy brow,
  For raptures visit me till now unfelt,
    And awe me with my boyhood's dream of God.

Glen Ellen.

LXV

ENCHANTMENT

Bind me with spells, O Lovely sorceress,
  And chain me with thy blessèd witchery!
  Never was there enchantress like to thee,
Whose triple power is wielded but to bless;
Nor of thy charm is there forgetfulness,
  Nor in thy kiss can any poison be:
  Thine instant lure is stronger than the sea,
And he thy wand has touched is ransomless.

Like wild, fresh winds that waft from Paradise
  Its holiness and fragrance, so is each
True word of thine! Lovers alone are wise,
  Of this mad world the only rightful lords;
So love me, thou who holdest in thy speech
  The clash of music's consecrated swords!

Glen Ellen.

LXVI

CORONATION

These fragile gifts I send thee, dearest dear—
  Three gathered leaves of ivy, orange, bay:
  The first in memory of that magic day
When first our clinging arms and lips drew near;
The second is for pledge of joy so sheer
  The very thought thereof is sweet dismay.
  Ah! Craig! Love leads us on a dazzling way
Whose rapture, not whose woe, I seem to fear!

But then that third, the fragrant laurel! There
  Is symbol of the recompense we hold
    For this grey world in which we gain such bliss.
Thence were the crowns that heroes bent to share,
  When, to the music of their Age of Gold,
    Pure on their brows fell Fame's transcendent kiss.

Glen Ellen.

LXVII

REVELATION

What mysteries can perfect love make plain!
  Lo! of two hearts' intrepid loneliness
  Love makes one Eden! Ere the midnight bless
My limbs with slumber, let thy face again
Flash on my soul its beatific pain,
  As bent above this golden, slender tress
  I tremble with thy beauty's dear excess,
And hunger for departed hours in vain.

Craig! it was part of *Thee!* My Love, it shone,
  Living and tremulous, on *Thy* dear head!
That head whose loveliness in hours unknown
      And vales untrod shall gleam upon my breast,
    Where lips may teach a thousand things unsaid,
      And blinding raptures lead us unto rest.

Glen Ellen.

LXVIII

ADORATION

Soon come the winter days, when white Altair
  Spreads wings above the sunset. Soon the snow,
  A fleeting seed the twilight heavens sow,
Descends from frigid levels of the air;
Chill grow the evenings we were born to share,
  And mute the hours wherein our souls might grow.
  Ah! make not Death our passion's afterglow,
Nor mix my final worship with despair!

Come soon, for soon a night is on our years,
  And soon the kissing lips have dust to taste!
  Love! I await thee with my flesh a flame.
Oh! breast to breast, and mouths a-salt with tears
  Of rending bliss, soon let us lie! Make haste!
  For music's heart is holy with thy name!

Glen Ellen.

LXIX

MY LOVE

In woman's dark and tedious war with Fate,
   Abide three comrades for her spirit mild:
   The mother, and the sweetheart, and the child.
Seldom the love maternal turns to hate,
The child's well nigh as seldom; but the mate
   Stands oft with forces passionate and wild,
   Not always to renouncement reconciled;
Not always loyal and compassionate.

All of a mother's love I cannot give,
   Yet somewhat of thy child I fain would be,
And as thy faithful lover always live,
     Be thou my star, and I will seek thy rays!
   Grant thou my heart a service but to thee,
     Thro' nights of rapture and achieving days!

Glen Ellen.

LXX

THE UNAVAILING

Alas! these mad monotonies I cry,
  Seeking for love a music and a speech,
  Striving in untranslated pain to teach
My soul a tongue that, living, could not die!
How mute the clouds and stars upon the sky,
  And yet how great their anthem! On the beach
  Toward hills that cannot hear the billows reach,
And hearing, changeless were the hills' reply.

Earth and her voices babble or are still:
  So must it be forever. If it be
    That Heaven awaits, and all the harps thereof,
In strains angelic half our thoughts must thrill,
  In songs celestial half our ecstasy,
    In that eternal music half our love!

Glen Ellen.

LXXI

LOVE'S PRIMACY

Love, the one holiness—shall I resist
  His all-consuming flame, and dare to think
  That thus my soul has broken any link
Of fleshly chains? For chains are all as mist
To those who turn from grosser chords to list
  Love's consecrating harmonies, and drink
  Where flowers tremble at his fountain's brink—
Pure as a lily that thy lips have kissed.

Nay! I will turn me to the evening stars
  (Some husht and jewelled dusk where roses die)
  And crave thy passion and the breath thereof,
Wasting my soul on Time's investing bars,
  And bearing in the heart thou makest high
  That pain which is the shadow cast by Love.

San Francisco.

LXXII

TO THY HEART

Believest thou in God? For sombre years
  I said: "He is not! If He be, His hand
  Is red with sinless blood, and His command
Decrees to man no harvest save of tears;
His angels wander hateful thro' the spheres,
  And we that hunger for a deathless land
  Pass like the foam upon the midnight sand!"
So to the stars I uttered half my fears.

So to the stars I stammered, full of dread.
  Then, as a star where mist has been before,
  Thy heavenly face within my heart was set,
And doubt befell my doubtings, and I said:
  "She is: shall not we be forevermore?
  And love? And God?" Alas! I know not yet!

Glen Ellen.

LXXIII

FROM TWO SKIES

Thou haunting loveliness and sweet despair!
  Thou art what music were, could music be
  A thing of form and tangibility!
Thou hast the morning hidden in thy hair,
And gleam of honey-colored moons that stare
  In evanescent twilights o'er the sea.
  As sorrow is to song art thou to me—
A thing of dews and flame, too sadly fair.

Thou callest to me out of time and space,
  And shinest with a glory from afar,
    A light and lure from never-charted skies,
And I exult, nor falter from thy face:
  My spirit seems a newly fallen star
    That flames upon thine own before it dies.

Oakland.

LXXIV

THE ABIDING PRESENCE

Surely our souls to each are ever near,
  Twain harps that mix one music; for to-day,
  As far in love's high reverie I lay,
One memory of thee, I seemed to hear
Thy voice within my breast—a chord so clear
  That as advancing seas the moon obey
  So the soul's waters trembled to thy sway,
Thy presence, Sweet, attested by a tear.

O great companionship! seraphic grief!
  O consecration and undying flame!
    Shall Sorrow breathe what mystery thou art?
Shall Love find here thy kiss, forlornly brief,
  Or speak the sense of worship in thy name,
    Told now in music to my haunted heart?

San Francisco.

LXXV

LOVE COMPLETE

Why know I words, since words must ever fail
  To tell thy loveliness and my despair?
  Why have I sight, with thee so more than fair,
And hearing, since I falter at the tale
Of thy perfection? Half I long to veil
  Each traitor sense ordaining that I share
  Love's sorrow, yet denying that I wear
His dearest lily, mystically pale.

Robed in his Dream, I worship and I yearn
  In toils of adoration and desire,
    Slave of thy flesh and vassal of thy soul,
Fain of thy snows and roses, as I burn
  With passion's splendor and the spirit's fire,
    Too sweet to shun, too cruel to control.

Carmel.

LXXVI

BY THE WESTERN OCEAN

Craig! Craig! my Love irradiant and divine!
  Here on the solitary sands I lie
  And see afar the lingering sunset die,
As peacefully its fading splendors shine
On western wave and on the eastern pine;
  And oh! to watch with thee that flaming sky,
  My heart one joy, one sacrament, one cry—
The heart whose very silences are thine!

The glory passes . . . Lo! the moon is up,
Remote and pure, that silvern, ancient cup
  From which earth drinks enchantment. Love! to be
  Its insubstantial pearl upon thy face!
  Ah! dearest! for an hour of thine embrace,
  Hushed by the deathless music of the sea!

Carmel.

LXXVII

A VISION

With dreams how splendid can the dark betray!
  Ere dawn, upon my right I saw thee stand,
  Foam of the silent seas of slumberland,
And lo! adoring, soon I heard thee say:
"I love thee as the poppies love the day,
  Which gone, they close, nor shall the moon's white hand
  Nor music of the choral stars expand
The bosoms faithful to the morning's ray."

Then, silence, as my vision in its stress
Broke with the passion of thy loveliness,
  And left my heart abandoned to the night.
    But ah! thine own at last shall guerdon me!
  Night hath her stars to grant, and Dawn her light,
    Spring hath her blossoms, and the future, *thee!*

Carmel.

LXXVIII

LOVE DESOLATE

So still and fragrant is the wood, O Sweet,
    I well could deem thy gracious presence near!
    Ah! God! an instant to behold thee here,
O beautiful, O goddess far and fleet!—
Thou in whose face the lures of legend meet,
    Thou in whose voice the lyres of old are clear,
    Who makest pain a joy, and sorrow dear,
And, by thine advent, Paradise complete!

Alas thy voice! its echo from the thrush
    Makes sad the tender silence following.
Alas thy face! for now the woodland hush
    Creeps to my heart, which, hopeless, seems to say:
    "She whom thou lovest is a vanished thing,
    A rose withdrawn, a planet lost in day."

Carmel.

LXXIX

THE PAIN OF BEAUTY

Often I wish thou wert less subtly fair!
That somewise fleck or slightest flaw might hold
  Thy beauty less than perfect—that the mold
Which held the goddess held not too my air.
Not Sappho with the roses in her hair,
  Nor Lilith naked in the moonlight cold,
  Nor Circe folded in the sunset's gold,
Wrought with their beauty so extreme despair.

O destined star my spirit sought from birth!
  Thy throne is light of worshipt heavens too high,
    Thy flame is made Infinity to me!
I watch thee, from this altar of the earth,
  As one who stands beneath a cloudless sky,
    And from a mountain gazes on the sea.

Carmel.

LXXX

A CONSTANCY OF SLEEP

Last night the sea put forth its utmost sigh,
 Making my soul aware of final things;
 And taking swift a dream-wind's mystic wings,
I seemed to pass to regions of the sky
That dome Arcadia and the bowers thereby,
 Wherein I saw the visions Homer sings,
 And nymphs abandoned to their wreathèd kings:
All these I saw, and saw them but to fly.

And fled, I cast their memory afar,
 True to that Heaven whereof thou livest star—
 Oh! star and wonder of what deeps of dream!
The murmur of the gods was in mine ears
 Like music's sorrow from immortal years,
 But past their bliss I saw thy features gleam.

Carmel.

LXXXI

DREAM'S ALCHEMY

Wakeful ere dawn, I heard the mighty sweep
  Of everlasting pinions on the night,
  And turned to mark with vision-litten sight
What visitants were mine from midnight's keep;
Whereat one spake, colossal: "I am Sleep."
  The other: "I am Love." In equal might
  They stood, twain gods of shadow and of light,
Flown from eternal turrets of the Deep.

Then, as I watched, uncertain whom to hold
  My spirits' lord, their majesties were blent,
The vans of darkness and the wings of gold,
    The breasts and brows of peace or ecstasy—
  One god and star on slumber's firmament,
    One mystery for lo! *I dreamt of thee!*

Carmel.

LXXXII

SOUL OF THE WORLD

Nature is made a shrine where I adore:
  My house of pines is murmurous of thee,
  As winds responsive wander from the sea.
The voice of ocean on the windy shore
Is like some god that calls thee. More and more
  The moonlight hath thy wands of witchery.
  Thy fragrance from the night is rendered me,
And thine the crown of stars Astarte wore.

But never dusk, nor the moon's white despair,
  Nor fragrances of star-restoring night,
    Nor hush when day and evening merge their hues,
Can ever wholly make my heart aware
  Of all thy spirit's lure and body's light,
    Too fair to keep, too marvelous to lose!

Carmel.

LXXXIII

DREAMLAND

Afar! afar! O Sweet, to fly afar,
   And drift entranced with dream-enfolded eyes
   In some inviolable Paradise,
Remote and hidden from the hands that mar
And laws of littleness that strive to bar
   Our breasts from love's divine and alien skies!
   To lie with love's own bliss, beyond surmise,
About our hearts as midnight round a star!

To watch the sea below intenser moons
   Whose lances tremble in abiding foams
      Or break to starlight in the ocean-maze,
And couched upon the silver of the dunes
   Bewitched to wait, the while my spirit roams
      The mad and irised Heaven of thy gaze!

San Francisco.

LXXXIV

THE SHADOW OF IMMORTALITY

Within the eternal music hast thou stood?
  Oh! tell me thou art mortal—it must be,
  Belovèd, thou art mortal, since to me
Who cannot know thy mystery if I would,
Thou dost comprise all thoughts of human good!
  Yet, in the dream God gives my soul of thee,
  Trembles a portent of Infinity,
And mystic glories touch thy womanhood.

Thine eyes seem part of Beauty's loneliness,
  Thy mouth her incommunicable flame,
    Thy voice the rapture of her star untrod
When chords ecstatic shudder with her stress—
  O thou the poignant music of whose name
    Is as a golden harpstring touched by God!

San Francisco.

LXXXV

UNTIL THOU COMEST

Now down the twilight floats the evening star,
  As sinks within my soul the thought of thee,
  O pearl far vanished in a futile sea!
O prisoner whom days unrisen bar!
Love, was thy holiness but made to mar,
  And all thy beauty given but to flee?
  Ah! darling! past my gaze thou waitest me,
For whose high soul my soul and worship are!

Now evening lies upon the western hill,
And thou art very distant from me still.
  The skies are made the turquoise court of day—
    The skies are made the sapphire court of night,
    And both are equal in my cheated sight,
  And each is bitter with our love's delay!

San Francisco.

LXXXVI

REBORN

What realms my memories of thee enfold!
  Never I read a tear-compelling tale
  Of queens that loved, or hero-vassaled grail,
But what the glimmer of thy locks of gold
Is on the heart's horizon, and I hold
  The paths of legend, clad in blessèd mail,
  Far-following thy shadow till it fail,
Or change to sorrow's star, forlornly cold.

Ah! Craig! and shall I lose thee? In thy face
  Meet all the visions, beautiful and sad,
    That woke man's hunger in the perished years,
When heroes travailed for a dream's embrace,
  And marshaled where the swords of death were glad,
    And sought thy lips beyond a thousand spears.

San Francisco.

LXXXVII

THE SILENT FANE

There needs no spoken word to tell the pain
  And constancy of this the love I feel:
  Let Dawn her rose or Night her stars conceal,
Or central ocean hide its purple stain,
And all that whisper vanish from the rain;
  But love, my love, must evermore reveal
  Its flame of consecration and appeal,
And live adoring, tho it live alone.

My life and love are one, forever one,
  An undivided worship at thy shrine,
And each a shade cast by thy spirit's sun.
   O love and silence! one in mystery,
  As star-companions one in splendor shine,
   Or wind and moonlight mix above the sea!

San Francisco.

LXXXVIII

THE LUTE-PLAYER

Then said I to the unassenting day:
  "Die swiftly!" And to Sleep: "Possess thou me,
  That thy nepenthe drug me utterly!
O hide thou me from Love, whose arrows slay
The peace for which I travail. Let my way
  Along the waters of oblivion be,
  And lead by Lethe to the ghostly sea
No star shall haunt nor moon of passion sway!"

So spake I in my sorrow. Now the night
  Lifts stars to make thy memory a pang,
The moon to hint thy mystery in light,
  And I am fain of Love and his despair.
  Return, O Day, the golden chords that rang,
    The aureate arrows and the yellow hair!

Carmel.

LXXXIX

THE HERITAGE OF THE SKIES

Time was when I could whisper to the wind:
  "Fly to my Sweet, and kiss her mouth and hair!"
  Or to a flower: "Go! she will deem thee fair,
Who is herself the fairest of her kind."
And if the rain to blossoms mute and blind
  Came like a benediction of the air,
  This too I felt we had the joy to share,
Or in an equal dusk its peace to find.

But now a farther eve enfolds thy grace,
And alien winds caress thy magic face—
  My flowers at last will reach thee sear and dead.
  But when the moon is white on eastern skies,
  Lo! on thy whiter brow her beams are shed!
    The selfsame stars make bright our tear-wet eyes!

Carmel.

XC

LOVE AND SORROW

O goddess of my pain! to-night I kneel
  Before thine altar, silent and alone.
  For woe like this shall ever joy atone?
On gloom like this shall ever morning steal?
In the rackt flesh the famished senses reel;
  The night that heard my rapture hears my moan
  And shadows haunt me from a hell unknown.
Aye! so a star might suffer could it feel!

All this must change, I know, since worlds must change:
  Sorrow at last must hush her mournful harp
    Or Lethe's dew be cold upon my breast;
But now the dark is terrible and strange;
  The sword of my despair is bleak and sharp,
    And all my soul one shudder of unrest!

Carmel.

XCI

IN VAIN

To what fair thing, O thou my Sweet!
 Shall best I liken thee?—
 Thou, white as where the sea
Breaks to the foam-flowers delicate and sweet!

Shall I go forth upon the wave
 To seek, perchance to find,
 Afar from sun and wind,
A moonlike pearl within an ocean cave?—

Then, clasping that, return and say:
 "Thou art more fair than this:
 Thy maiden bosom is
More white than snows beneath the moon or day?"

And then, should not I yearn to cry:
 "Thy forehead is as white,
 Oh! and thine eyes' strange light
Sweeter than any stars that take the sky?"

But thou, I dream, wouldst silent stand
 With those great eyes of thine,
 Young, exquisite, divine,
Turned for a moment on my trembling hand,

And smile a little sadly, till
 I knew my gift in vain,
 And all for naught the pain
Whose tears of love my hopeless eyes should fill!

Carmel.

XCII

THE HIDDEN GODDESS

Thou hast been human ever. None the less,
  It seemed a captive radiance in thee slept,
  Not all of earth—a mystic light that leapt
Within thine eyes, which could not all suppress
Their heavenly betrayal, nor confess
  What spirit stirred within their deeps and kept
  Angelic wardenship of tears unwept—
A subtle, wild and starry loveliness.

Sweet, thou dost lift my soul to breathless heights.
  Some beauty once I cherished, but thou hast
Been moon of unimaginable nights.
  Beauty I knew, but how could I know thee?
  For, till their eyes behold its waves at last,
  The desert-born imagine not the sea.

Carmel.

XCIII

LOVE'S MERCY

The pains of Love are terrible and sweet!
  Let countless men in all their days and lands
  Appraise the gods, whether where Thule's sands
Debar the sea, or Egypt's weary feet
Pause for a night at Ammon's royal seat—
  They shall find Love the lord of all. He stands
  With heart unsparing and resistless hands,
Whose grace the mortals and the gods entreat.

Alas his snares made cunning to enmesh!
  His whispers of thy passion that as whips
Scourge at the midnight my tormented flesh;
    Till flesh and soul stand equal in their flame!
  O sovereign compassion of his lips,
    That make the morning holy with thy name!

Carmel.

XCIV

SONG'S FUTILITY

'Tis but the ghost of beauty that I bring:
  Of star and moon, of twilight and the flow'r,
  Of Music in her lone, unhappy hour,
I give thee gleam and echo, offering
But shadows of the loveliness I sing.
  So must it be: it lies beyond Art's pow'r
  To pluck the central rose of Beauty's bow'r;
Her deeper heavens defy his eager wing.

Of what avail my worship and its grief,
  As now I strain the bonds of speech, and long
  To find a thousand ways to call thee fair,
Except beyond the words thou find belief,
  Beyond belief, the heart that breaks with song,
  Beyond the song, Love's silences to share?

Carmel.

XCV

AT SUNSET

Loose now thy flaming pinions on the West,
   Vega, thou heavenly lamp of my desire!
   Now burns the sun upon its crimson pyre,
Based on the windless Islands of the Blest;
The mountains now are purple to the crest.
   Oh! crown the dying sunset with thy fire,
   And stir the sleeping music of the Lyre
To ardencies of silvery unrest!

Aye! with thy quiring charm the vacant night!
   But in my heart are chords that one alone
     Can move to gracious harmonies untold.
Musing on her, I gaze beyond thy light,
   Until my soul seems filled with harps that moan,
     Strung by the seraphs with her hair of gold.

Carmel.

XCVI

THE IMMORTAL

Oh! sad or sweet are all the lapsing days,
  The days that crown themselves with stars, and die;
  And sweet the sea-wind's unenduring sigh,
Or morning larks' involuntary lays,
Deep cut in music's crystal. Green the ways
  On which the feet of Spring to Summer fly;
  But song and wind and hue, we know not why,
Pass, and the very stars put by their rays.

Transition is upon the ancient skies
  And change upon the mountain's granite brow;
No life is fashioned but another dies,
  No splendor given unto earth but we
  Regret at last its close: thou, only thou,
  Dost give me dreams of immortality.

Carmel.

XCVII

BLOSSOM OR BIRD

Darling, thy form and fragrance haunt the Spring,
  And every wind becomes thy messenger;
    To whisperings of thee the woodlands stir,
And waves from out the western ocean bring
A freight of foam that leaves me wondering,
  Who know thy bosom is as white. O spur
    Of Spring, when every bird's a sorcerer,
And jonquils waken as the linnets sing!

Oh! Craig! it seems that Spring's transmuting word
Should turn each lifted flower to a bird,
    Till all should flutter to thee where thou art;
      Or else that every blossom should attain
      The morning linnet's gift of song, and rain
    A fragrant music on thy listening heart.

Carmel.

XCVIII

LONGING

Why standest thou on Beauty's topmost peak,
  So distant that the very stars appear
  Thy coronal irradiant and near?
Why standest there, with all my heart too weak
Ever to dream that silent Fate shall speak
  The words I wait forevermore to hear,
  Foredoomed to reckon Beauty's rose too dear
And find its throne upon thine either cheek?

What tho I stand so close its perfumed dart
  Slays sleep itself? Unclaspt thou still must go,
As each year steals a petal from its heart,
    Till on the face where Love's mad lips would feed
  Death's snows are set to match thy spirit's snow—
    Thou'rt lost, and every other flower's a weed!

Carmel.

XCIX

THE NEW GODDESS

Time was, indeed, O first of all things fair!
  When Nature stood in queenship of my breast:
  Full-tenderly she led the winds to rest,
And flowers and dews were witness of her care;
I seemed to hear her whispers everywhere;
  The very heavens were lit at her behest,
  As tho' with lifted wings upon the West
A seraph clove the crimson-flooded air.

But now the mighty sunsets flare in vain,
And winds allegiant strew the mournful rain;
  Because of thee my heart is hungered fire.
    Alas! I wander at the land's extreme,
  Lost in irresolutions of desire
    And torn by hopes that gods might dread to dream!

Carmel.

C

TO THE MOON

Loose me thy pearl, O empress of the night!
  And with thy scattered silver purchase me
  The freedoms of celestial sorcery;
For I would worship, far from mortal sight,
My marvellous, my lady of delight.
  So gleam, and by thy lustre I shall see
  Hope's eager smile, and Rapture's breast made free,
And Love more fey and exquisite and white.

Nay! loose thy spell, thy radiant charm annul!
  Alas! thou seemest near and she remote!
    There drifts unhappy magic on thy beams—
Madness and pain, for now, invisible,
  Soft-handed Passion grips my straining throat
    And shows her beautiful beyond my dreams.

Oakland.

CI

LOST IN LIGHT

From citadels of dream I turn to see
  How high the Morning builds her golden wall.
  O city of the light! how purely fall
The jewels of thy far tranquillity,
Tho now thy glories but restore to me
  The desert of my loneliness, nor all
  The lure and grace of her whom now I call
Vainly as night its starshine lost in thee!

O goddess far for whom I know no bond!
O tears within the music! Face beyond
  The sunset fallen on enchanted lands!
    O wine no lips of passion may consume!
  Return, O night! and with immortal hands
    Rebuild for Love thy palaces of gloom!

Carmel.

CII

THE PATH TO PARADISE

Of all that tapestry which is the past,
   Sweet, I would change no slightest hue nor thread;
   For little tho the change, my feet were led
Thereby to altars other than thou hast.
Ah God! how small a step, and I, outcast,
   Had never seen the rays of splendor shed
   From Love's uplifted and refulgent head,
Nor stood within thy spirit's light at last.

And so there is no pain I do not bless,
   Nor any hunger thou dost not suffice;
Nor would I have life's scheme one woe the less,
    Since such have led from nothingness to thee,
   Whom lacking, I had won not Paradise,
    Nor evermore Love's all and ecstasy.

San Francisco.

INDEX OF FIRST LINES